DIABETES

DIABETES

ELIZABETH FERBER

The Millbrook Medical
Library

The Millbrook Press
Brookfield, Connecticut

Library of Congress Cataloging–in–Publication Data
Ferber, Elizabeth, 1967–
Diabetes / Elizabeth Ferber.
p.   cm.— (The Millbrook medical library)
Includes bibliographical references and index.
Summary: Explanation of the nature of diabetes, the various forms
of treatment, and the many physical and emotional challenges faced by
children and young adults who live with this disease. Contains case studies
and interviews of young people ages eight through twenty-five. Further
reading, sources, and index included.
ISBN 1-56294-655-2 (lib. bdg.)
1. Diabetes—Juvenile literature. I. Title. II. Series.
RC660.5F47   1996
616.4'62—dc20 96-5173 CIP

Photographs courtesy of Stock, Boston: pp. 17 (Elizabeth Crews),
23 (John Coletti), 29 (Billy E. Barnes), 41, 47 (David Carmack),
57 (Jean-Claude LeJeune), 66 (Bob Daemmrich), 75 (John Lei);
Photo Researchers: pp. 34 (Will & Deni McIntyre), 69 (Rita Nannini),
83 (Mark C. Burnett). Diagrams by Frank Senyk.

Published by The Millbrook Press, Inc.
Brookfield, Connecticut

For Nancy

CONTENTS

FOREWORD

Type I diabetes, or insulin-dependent diabetes mellitus, formally known as juvenile-onset diabetes mellitus, is the most common hormonal problem in children and adolescents. Until 1921, when insulin, a hormone secreted by the pancreas, was first isolated and then used as a drug, diabetes was almost universally fatal within two years of diagnosis. When it was discovered, it was hoped that insulin would "cure" diabetes, as administration of other hormones cured the diseases caused by their absence (hypothyroidism, for instance, is cured by oral supplements of the hormone l-thyroxine). Unhappily, within a decade, it became evident that injected insulin was not a cure for diabetes. Until as recently as 1993, there had been constant debate about what normal blood-sugar levels should be in the average person.

We hope that in the next few years better treatment of or a cure for diabetes will be found. Until then, controlling diabetes is the best hope for teenagers with diabetes. Multiple blood tests, basically three to four per day, enable the patient and doctor to choose the insulin doses more accurately. Blood sugar can also be tested with blood-glucose tests. Blood-glucose monitoring, including home tests, have greatly improved diabetes care. Noninvasive blood-glucose testing (that is, made through the skin without drawing blood) may soon be available and make it even easier to take many measurements.

Elizabeth Ferber has interviewed doctors and patients and put their remarks and medical knowledge into an easily readable form. The social and emotional aspects of adolescence often have an enormous impact on the treatment of diabetes, and the author's use of patients' remarks is particularly important. While there have been many books written for patients with diabetes, this useful book has been written especially for teenagers and their families.

Fredda Ginsberg-Fellner, M.D.
Professor of Pediatrics
Director, Division of Pediatric
Endocrinology and Metabolism
Mt. Sinai Medical Center
New York

WHO'S WHO

Nine young people who are living with diabetes were generous enough with their time and courageous enough with their spirits to share their stories with you. In this book, you'll hear them describe in their own words what it's like to cope with a chronic illness like diabetes through childhood and through the period of adolescence, which presents its own special challenges. They hope their experiences will inspire as well as teach you.

Nora, 25 years old
Nora found out she had diabetes when she was just eleven years old. She remembers that her first question to the doctor who diagnosed her was, "Will I be able to have a baby someday?" She also remembers the struggle she had throughout her adolescence, when she suffered from a severe eating disorder. Today, fourteen years later, Nora is a healthy young mother of a one-year-old son named Steven.

Rachel, 11 years old
Now an avid gymnast, Rachel received the news that she had diabetes before she was six years old. At first, she found all the rules about her eating and physical activities overwhelming. But now that she knows how to give herself her medicine and test her own blood-sugar levels, she is able to play all the sports she wants and even spend weekends away from home.

Abigail, 10 years old
Abigail says that the hardest thing about having diabetes is not being able to eat birthday cake. Diagnosed at the age of four, Abigail thinks that telling her friends and classmates all about what it's like to have diabetes has helped her to feel that she fits in and is part of the crowd.

Mark, 12 years old
Mark is happiest when he's tossing a football or kicking a soccer ball down a field. He says that one of the biggest challenges about having diabetes is not eating candy with all of his friends at school. When he was eleven, he made a video with a few friends describing what it was like to have diabetes, which he feels taught him as much as it has taught others.

Susan, 13 years old
Last summer, when Susan was twelve, she spent her first summer at a camp for girls with diabetes. She had such a good time that she's going again next summer. The best thing about it, she says, is that she gets to do the very same things at her camp that her twin sister, who does not have diabetes, does at the camp she attends.

Bonnie, 14 years old
Bonnie, who loves to travel, recently took a trip across the United States with a group of teenagers all about her age. She had a terrific time until she got the flu and had to

leave for home. Sometimes, she says, her diabetes can make a simple case of the flu into a big deal. Although she and her sister have a great relationship now, Bonnie remembers that her sister used to be very jealous over all the attention Bonnie first received from her parents when she was diagnosed with diabetes at the age of six.

Robert, 15 years old

The most frustrating thing about having diabetes, says Robert, is trying to keep his diet, exercise, and medication regimen in control. No matter how hard he tries, it seems that his blood sugar still swings from high to low and back again, especially in the middle of the night. Robert is determined, however, not to let his diabetes get in the way of his dream to become a professional basketball player.

Amanda, 8 years old

Amanda remembers how scary it was when she first went to the hospital for her diabetes. Since then, she's learned about the disease and how to care for herself. She doesn't mind telling other people, including her friends, about diabetes, but she is still sometimes afraid that they might laugh at her.

Katie, 15 years old

Katie's goal is to become an actress. She also loves to ride horses and go to dance clubs. Sometimes she wishes that she did not have to think so much about her diabetes, but she realizes that when she takes good care of herself, she feels better physically and emotionally. She has a new exercise program that is helping her to keep her blood-sugar levels under control and her body in good shape.

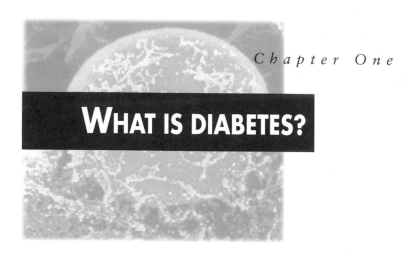

WHAT IS DIABETES?

RACHEL'S STORY

As six-year-old Rachel watched her parents prepare for a trip to celebrate their tenth wedding anniversary, she began to feel very tired and ill. She had been suffering with a mild cold for about a week, and on November 15, 1990, her cold became worse and she found it difficult to get out of bed. Her parents planned to leave the next morning, but when her mother noticed that she had eaten three bowls of cereal and had drunk twelve glasses of water without stopping, she became quite concerned. In addition, Rachel's cold showed no signs of letting up. Her parents, Elise and Robert, decided to postpone their trip and take Rachel to the pediatrician.

Rachel remembers being a little nervous when she arrived at the doctor's office, but he reassured her that she would be okay. He administered some *tests—taking some blood and some urine—that told him all he needed to know about what was making Rachel feel so sick. He told Rachel and her parents that she had Type I diabetes, a type of endocrine (glandular) disorder.*

Rachel was very scared when she first heard about the disease. She had had a few illnesses as a young child, like chicken pox and the mumps, but both of them went away within a few days. It was hard for Rachel to understand that diabetes would be with her forever.

Yet, while there was a great deal for her to learn at first, Rachel felt reassured that she would not have to deal with everything all at once. There were many aspects of diabetes—including how to lead a healthy and active life while controlling the disease—that she would learn over the next few years, and over the course of her life.

That night, her doctor admitted her to the hospital for a week-long stay. Slowly but surely, during that week, she and her parents began understand what was happening to her. "I felt very alone when I first went to the hospital, and I was scared I would never lead a normal life," Rachel remembers. "I didn't know if I could ever eat junk food or play sports with my friends. My doctor told me and my parents that I could. By the time I left the hospital, I knew how hard my life would be, but I also knew it wasn't the end of the world."

UNDERSTANDING DIABETES

Diabetes is a chronic illness, which means that it has no cure and has symptoms that persist over a long period of time. Except in the most rare and severe of cases, diabetes is not fatal, but people with diabetes must treat their condition every day or they risk becoming very ill. Like most other kinds of chronic illnesses, including arthritis and epilepsy, the course of diabetes is unpredictable. Everyone with the condition has a different experience with it: Some people take very good care of themselves but nevertheless eventually develop life-threatening complications. Other people pay less attention to maintaining their health but are lucky enough to avoid serious problems.

In general, however, how well people with diabetes take care of themselves greatly affects the short-and long-term symptoms and side effects related to this condition. Young people with diabetes have limits imposed upon them by the disease. If they eat properly, exercise regularly, and take their insulin, however, these young people will be able to enjoy the same activities and realize as many dreams as their peers.

Diabetes is one of the most common chronic illnesses in the United States. About 16 million Americans have diabetes, and about 5 percent (about 800,000) are young people diagnosed with Type I. Diabetes is a serious condition, one that a person must cope with every day for the rest of his or her life.

APPROXIMATELY 16 MILLION PEOPLE IN THE UNITED STATES HAVE DIABETES. FIVE PERCENT OF THIS NUMBER, OR ABOUT 800,000, HAVE A TYPE OF DIABETES CALLED TYPE I. MOST YOUNG PEOPLE WITH DIABETES HAVE THIS FORM OF THE DISEASE, WHICH USUALLY DEVELOPS BETWEEN THE AGES OF NINE AND THIRTY.

The medical term for diabetes is diabetes mellitus, a phrase derived from two ancient languages. The word *diabetes* comes from a combination of two Greek words meaning "siphon" or "run through." This term describes the enormous loss of water through urine that is one of the

With proper diet, regular exercise, and the necessary medical attention, most young people with diabetes can lead active, healthy lives—and play any kind of sport they wish.

major symptoms of the onset of diabetes. After discovering that urine contained a high quantity of sugar, the Romans added the word *mellitus,* which means "honey" in Latin. Loosely translated, then, diabetes mellitus means "a running through of sugar."

To understand what it means to have diabetes, you need to understand what goes wrong in the body of a person with diabetes. Diabetes is a condition in which the body is unable to process sugars and starches—also called carbohydrates—into glucose, the body's principal source of energy. The disease develops when specific cells in the pancreas—a gland located in the abdomen near the stom-

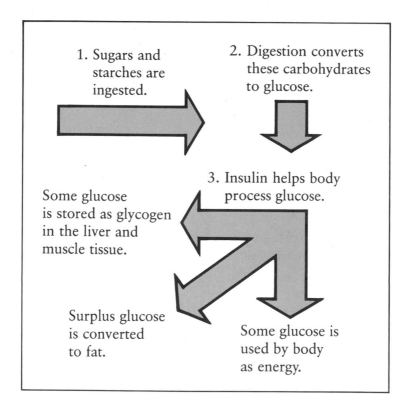

Conversion of carbohydrates to glucose to glycogen.

ach—is unable to produce a hormone called insulin, or when the body is unable to use insulin properly. The cells in the pancreas that produce insulin are called beta cells.

Normally, the level of glucose in the blood rises after a person eats a meal. This rise in blood glucose stimulates the beta cells to release insulin. Insulin then either helps body cells take up glucose to use as energy or promotes the conversion of glucose to fat (which can be used by cells later). Some glucose may also be stored in the liver as a substance called glycogen. Then, when the level of glucose drops (usually several hours after the meal has been eaten), other cells in the pancreas stimulate the conversion of glycogen to glucose and its release into the bloodstream. In this way, the level of glucose in the bloodstream stays relatively constant until the next meal is eaten.

In people who have diabetes, either the beta cells do not produce enough insulin or the body cannot use insulin properly. Without insulin, glucose cannot enter cells, and its level in the blood rises. When this occurs, body cells are essentially starved of their fuel, and a series of events takes place that cause the symptoms that define the condition of diabetes.

THE TWO TYPES OF DIABETES

Scientists have identified two different kinds of diabetes, Type I or insulin-dependent diabetes, and Type II or non-insulin-dependent diabetes.

- *Type I (insulin-dependent):* Type I diabetes occurs when the pancreas produces little or no insulin. Ten percent of people with diabetes have Type I diabetes. Type I diabetes is also known as juvenile diabetes because most people develop the condition during childhood or adolescence. Most people with Type I diabetes must take insulin on a daily basis, which is why the condition is also called insulin-dependent diabetes. The insulin is injected beneath the skin into the tissue. Without it, the body cannot function properly.

• *Type II (non-insulin-dependent):* Type II diabetes, also called adult-onset diabetes, is the most common form of the illness. About 80 to 90 percent of Americans with diabetes have this form, and the majority of them develop the disease after the age of forty. In this type of diabetes the pancreas still produces insulin, but either the pancreas does not produce enough of the hormone or the body does not use it in an efficient way. As a result, the insulin fails to do its job. Like those with Type I diabetes, people with Type II suffer from high levels of circulating glucose, which may create serious health problems.

TYPES OF DIABETES		
	Type I	*Type II*
Percentage of all people with diabetes	10 to 15 percent	85 to 90 percent
Age of diagnosis	usually under 30	usually over 40
Weight of patient	often thin or normal weight	often overweight
General treatment	insulin injections, diet, and exercise	diet, exercise, and, if needed, oral agents or insulin
Onset of symptoms	usually sudden, very apparent	gradual and often subtle

WHAT CAUSES DIABETES?

Although it is still unclear exactly what causes diabetes, doctors and scientists believe that there are a number of possible causes:

- *Viruses:* The results of extensive research show that certain viruses (disease-causing microorganisms) may infect the pancreas, reducing or destroying its ability to produce insulin.

- *Autoimmune disorder:* Scientists believe that in some cases the body's own defense system—called the immune system—destroys beta cells. They do not, however, fully understand why the immune system, which normally protects the body from harmful foreign substances such as bacteria and viruses, turns against healthy cells. One theory suggests that a viral infection triggers the immune system, which then mistakenly attacks beta cells as well as the virus.

- *Genetics:* Diabetes—especially Type II diabetes—tends to develop in people with a family history of the disorder. Along with other traits, such as eye color and height, parents can also pass on certain characteristics that may predispose their children to develop diabetes. In the case of Type I diabetes, scientists believe that if a father has diabetes, his children have a 5 to 10 percent chance of developing the disorder before the age of twenty. If a mother has Type I diabetes, the children have half the risk, a 2 to 5 percent chance of developing the illness.

  In addition, the risk of developing Type I diabetes increases with the number of relatives affected. For example, if one sibling has Type I diabetes, there is only a small risk that a brother or sister will have it, too; however, if two siblings have Type I diabetes, the risk of a third sibling developing the disease rises to 10 percent.

  For Type II diabetes, the genetic link is even stronger. If one parent has this condition, his or her child has as much as a 25 to 30 percent chance of developing the disease. If both parents have Type II, the risk of inheriting the illness rises to nearly 75 percent.

• *Stress:* Scientists strongly believe that the onset of diabetes may be triggered by one or many forms of stress in the body. These can include surgical operations, a serious accident or injury, and even an emotional trauma, such as a divorce or a death in the family.

SYMPTOMS AND COMPLICATIONS

When a person first develops diabetes, several symptoms may appear. Rachel, for instance, exhibited most of the classic symptoms even before her parents noticed that she was ill. As her condition worsened, Rachel began to drink and urinate excessively. She seemed to be always hungry, crave sweet foods, and feel sick and weak. Despite her increased appetite and eating patterns, Rachel continued to lose weight in the weeks before her diagnosis.

SOME OF THE MOST COMMON SIGNS OF DIABETES:

• **EXCESSIVE THIRST AND HUNGER**
• **EXCESSIVE URINATION**
• **EXHAUSTION**
• **FLU AND COLDLIKE SYMPTOMS**

Why are fatigue, hunger, and thirst symptoms of diabetes? How can someone lose weight even when eating the same amount of food—or more? Because glucose cannot enter the cells of the body of a person with diabetes, the cells are deprived of energy, which causes the person to feel physical exhaustion. When the body senses that the cells lack glucose, it craves more food. Even when food is consumed, however, the cells are unable to get the amount of energy they need.

Frequent and heavy urination is another common symptom of diabetes. The kidneys begin to work extra hard to eliminate some of the excess sugar by expelling it through urine. As the body becomes dehydrated through

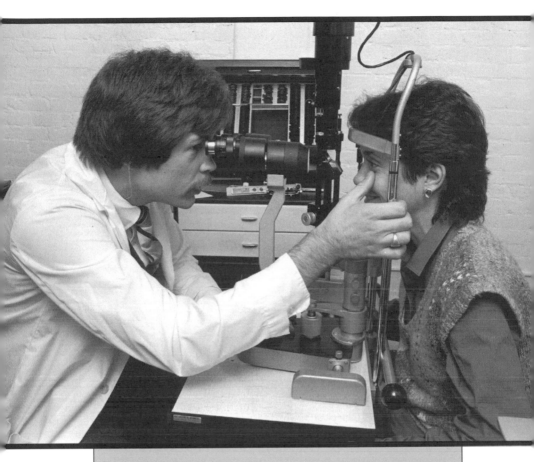

Unless diabetes is properly treated and monitored, it can lead to several other conditions, including an eye disease known as retinopathy.

this process, it craves more fluid, and the person with diabetes suffers from great thirst, just as Rachel did.

Other Conditions Related to Diabetes

Diabetes is a highly manageable disease, and those who have it and are treated for it can almost always expect to live healthy, normal lives. Nevertheless, having high levels of glucose in your bloodstream over long periods of time may eventually cause some problems.

- *Neuropathy* is nerve damage caused by high blood pressure. It occurs when glucose invades certain nerve cells, causing them to swell. This results in feelings of tingling, loss of sensation, and/or pain.

- *Cardiovascular disease* is the leading cause of death among diabetic patients. Exactly why diabetes adversely affects the cardiovascular system is unknown, but those with diabetes run a much higher risk of developing heart disease and high blood pressure.

- *Retinopathy* is a serious eye disease that occurs when blood vessels in the eyes become weak, causing fluid to leak from them. When fluid leaks into the retina—the thin inner lining of the eye—the vision blurs. If the disease progresses, blindness may occur.

- *Nephropathy* occurs when tiny blood vessels in the kidneys are damaged by high blood-glucose levels.

Generally, these problems do not affect adolescents or young adults, because it usually takes many years for high blood-glucose levels to cause damage. Nevertheless, they reveal how important it is for all people with diabetes to take special care to control their disease.

If a person with diabetes is not treated for the condition, there can be other serious complications in addition to these common problems. For example, in people with Type I diabetes, a condition known as ketoacidosis may occur. A lack of insulin in the blood (and hence high levels of blood glucose) triggers the body to turn to its fat stores for energy. When this occurs, the body burns the fatty acids into substances called ketones. When too many ketones accumulate in the blood, the blood becomes more acid. In extreme cases, ketoacidosis can lead to coma (called diabetic coma) and even death.

DAILY TREATMENTS FOR DIABETES

When a person is first diagnosed with diabetes, his or her blood sugar is often already dangerously high. The first priority is to lower the blood sugar quickly so that no serious complications—such as a diabetic coma—can ensue. Once out of immediate danger, the person can then learn how to treat diabetes on a day-to-day basis. Daily treatment consists of three main components:

- *Insulin injections:* Most people with Type I diabetes must inject insulin on a daily basis. The insulin is injected beneath the skin into the body's tissues from one to three times a day (sometimes more often). In addition, these people must learn to monitor their blood-sugar levels by taking a simple blood test one or more times a day.

- *Diet:* The second most important aspect of treatment is controlling the amount of carbohydrates and sugar eaten during the day. The goal is to match the amount of glucose entering the body to the amount of insulin injected. To do so, people with diabetes must be aware of how much food they eat and when they eat it.

- *Exercise:* Exercise is the third part of treatment for Type I diabetes. Exercise is important for two reasons: First, getting regular exercise is essential to good health for everyone, whether a person has diabetes or not. Second, physical activity appears to help muscle cells take up and use sugar even when there are lower levels of insulin in the blood. This helps to keep cells nourished and blood-glucose levels normal. The amount and timing of exercise are extremely important for someone with Type I diabetes, however, as discussed in Chapter 3. Generally, the more active a person is, the more glucose the body's cells require, so the person does not need to inject as much insulin.

In fact, according to Dr. Fredda Ginsberg-Fellner, Chief of Pediatric Endocrinology at Mt. Sinai Medical Center in New York City, "control is the word" that many people with diabetes say defines their daily life. Every day, people with diabetes must plan carefully what they will eat and when they will eat it, how much exercise they can tolerate, and if they are taking the right amount of insulin. Only by maintaining what is known as "good" control—a safe blood-glucose level—can young people with diabetes help prevent complications from developing.

In this book, several people will describe how they felt when they first heard that they had diabetes and how they eventually learned how to cope with the challenges the disease presents. As you read their stories and learn more about the treatments available, you'll discover as they did that diabetes often becomes easier to manage over time.

DIAGNOSIS AND TREATMENT

NORA'S STORY

On my eleventh birthday, my life completely changed forever. That was the day I learned I had diabetes.

It all started a few weeks before, on the night that my family went out to dinner to congratulate my sister for making the cheerleading squad at school. At dinner, I drank seven people's waters, seven people's soda, everybody's refills, and even then I was still thirsty. And every few seconds I had to go to the bathroom.

I felt like that—thirsty and like I had to use the bathroom all the time—for a few weeks. I kept thinking it would go away, but it didn't. I also felt weak and a little sick. My mother started to worry when she noticed I'd lost a lot of weight. She was afraid that I might have a urinary tract infection or something like that. Finally, I was feeling so sick on my birthday that my mother brought me to the *emergency room at the hospital and called my pediatrician. The doctor asked me all kinds of questions about how I was feeling, how much I ate and drank, and if anything else was bothering me. He took some blood from my arm and told me to wait with my mother in the hospital room.*

A few hours later, he came back and told us that I had diabetes. He suggested that I stay in the hospital and work with the nurses and doctors there to learn about the disease and how I would have to care for myself. I was really scared at first, and I don't think I could have gotten through it without my mother.

About a week later, I left the hospital, complete with a set of disposable syringes, a diet and exercise plan, and the phone numbers of doctors and support groups that I could call anytime. I still had my worries, but I knew I'd be okay.

RECEIVING THE DIAGNOSIS

Although everyone experiences diabetes in a different way, many young people share similar memories of receiving their diagnosis. Fifteen-year-old Robert recalls: "I was diagnosed in the middle of fifth grade. My mom, who also has diabetes, noticed that I was drinking a lot of water, so she brought me to the doctor right away. When I first heard what was wrong, I thought 'What a drag' and I was a little scared. But it hasn't turned out to be so bad. You get used to it."

Most people receive their diagnoses when they are still young, so that their parents must play a pivotal role in their care. However, even if parents are involved, diagnosis and the months immediately following it can be very uncertain and frightening. Rachel, who is eleven, was diagnosed at the age of six. She remembers: "I was very nervous at first about giving myself shots. I couldn't stand the

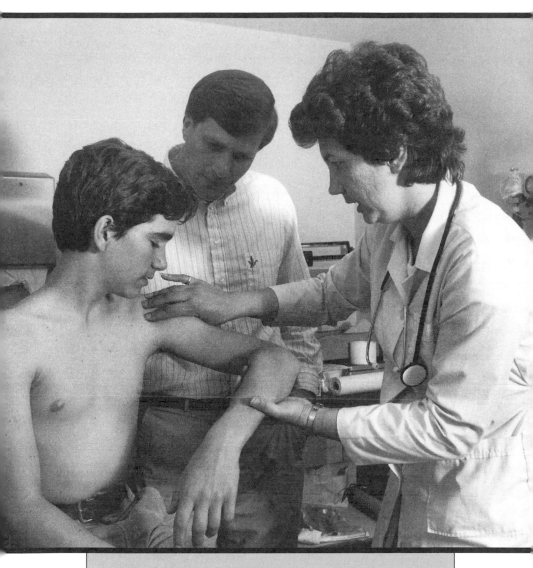

A medical team of social workers, physicians, and psychologists can help parents and young people with diabetes learn how to live with and manage the condition.

idea of putting a needle in my body every day. The shots, though, aren't the hard part anymore. It's the constant testing of my blood sugar that is the bigger pain."

Ten-year-old Abigail has an even longer history of coping with diabetes. "I was only four when I found out I had diabetes. I don't remember much about what happened, except that the nurses were really nice to me at the hospital. Now, diabetes is just another part of my life. I have to think about it all the time, but it seems normal. It's all I've ever known."

The immediate task for the newly diagnosed person and his or her family is to learn as much as possible about the disease. Because a diagnosis of diabetes raises so many questions for both young people and their parents, it is very important for a newly diagnosed person to work with a team of medical professionals to address both the physical and emotional challenges related to the disease. Melissa Strugger is a social worker and a member of the medical team at Mt. Sinai Hospital in New York City called The Carole and Michael Friedman and Family Young People's Diabetes Treatment Unit. She counsels people with diabetes and their families when they are first diagnosed and often for many years after.

Ms. Strugger believes that when people are first told they have diabetes they are usually in need of comfort and advice. Initially, she tells her young patients and their parents what will happen in the hospital and what they can expect once they go home. When people are first diagnosed, they usually have many questions about how diabetes will affect their lives. Social workers and psychologists are the members of the medical team that can help the learning process begin.

THE MEDICAL TEAM

Like Nora, most young people are very sick when they are first diagnosed with diabetes. They must stay in a hospital until doctors can stabilize their conditions by lowering their blood sugar with injections of insulin. An endocrinologist—a doctor who specializes in hormone-related disorders, including diabetes—is usually the person in charge of this care. Sometimes the young person's regular doctor, usually a pediatrician, provides the diagnosis and designs a treatment plan. Most experts, however, recommend that young people with diabetes be evaluated by an endocrinologist at some point to ensure that they are receiving the best treatment possible for their condition.

Nora had a team of professionals who took care of her in her hometown of St. Louis, Missouri, during the first few years after her diagnosis. "It wasn't until I moved away and began to see a doctor somewhere else that I realized how lucky I was to have been treated through a team approach."

The medical team that works together to help young people learn to cope with diabetes usually includes endocrinologists, pediatricians, nurses, dieticians, and social workers. While doctors usually concentrate on the medical needs of people with diabetes, other members of the team can provide ongoing counseling and care. The medical team often becomes like another family to those with diabetes.

During and after the initial hospitalization, the medical team teaches the basics of diabetes care to the patient and his or her family. How much information they impart depends on how old the patient is and how mature he or she seems to the medical team. As hard as doctors and nurses might try to make the condition and treatment procedures easy to understand, young people may feel overwhelmed by all they need to learn. Katie, another diabetes patient, says: "I think doctors and other medical professionals have to realize that you're not a doctor and that they have to explain treatment in terms you can understand and that won't be too upsetting at first. It's very easy to panic when you first hear about all the things you have to do."

INSULIN: THE CORNERSTONE
OF TREATMENT

As described in Chapter 1, treatment of diabetes consists of three basic components: insulin replacement, diet, and exercise.

When people are diagnosed with diabetes, one of the first new words they learn is *insulin*. Insulin is a hormone, a chemical released by a gland into the bloodstream in order to stimulate a certain body function. This hormone, which is produced by the pancreas, controls the conversion of carbohydrates, proteins, and fats into glucose. Once glucose enters body cells, it is burned as energy. Insulin also transforms glucose into glycogen, a form of energy stored in liver and muscle tissue and used whenever the body runs short of glucose.

People with Type I diabetes are unable to produce their own insulin, and rely instead on insulin that is manufactured outside the body. This insulin is injected into the fatty tissue of the skin and then absorbed into the bloodstream. The goal of insulin treatment is to provide enough insulin for the body to be able to use the glucose derived from food in an efficient way.

Types of Insulin

All insulin produced in the United States was at one time made from insulin that had been extracted from the pancreases of cattle and pigs. Unfortunately, this insulin was filled with impurities that sometimes upset the systems of those who injected it. Today, insulin is available in two forms—a semisynthetic form made by converting pork insulin into a form that is basically identical to human insulin, and recombinant insulin, a form that is also basically identical to human insulin made through genetic engineering. (Genetic engineering is the manipulation of genes from animals or plants in a laboratory.) A doctor decides which form of manufactured insulin is best for each diabetes patient.

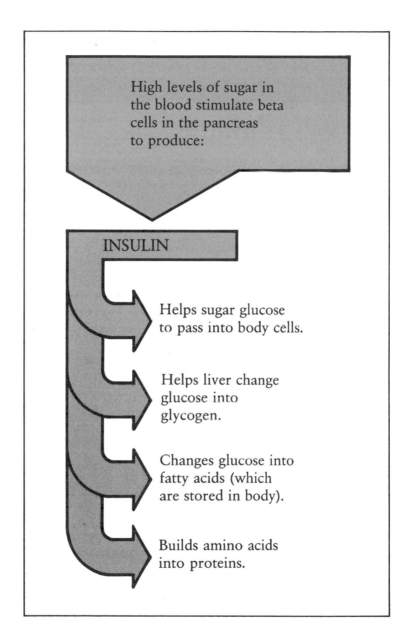

High levels of sugar in the blood stimulate beta cells in the pancreas to produce:

INSULIN

Helps sugar glucose to pass into body cells.

Helps liver change glucose into glycogen.

Changes glucose into fatty acids (which are stored in body).

Builds amino acids into proteins.

Production of insulin in the pancreas and release into the body.

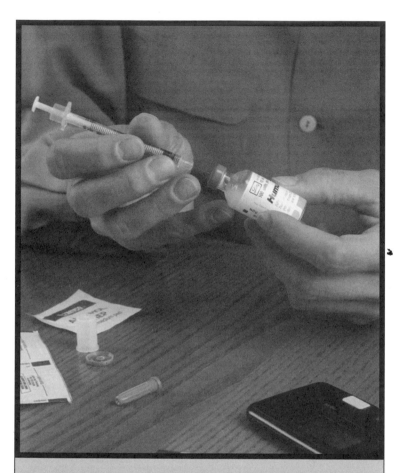

People who have diabetes either do not produce enough of the hormone insulin or their bodies cannot use it properly. To compensate, those with Type I diabetes rely on daily injections of one of three types of manufactured insulin, or a combination of types.

Although there are two ways of manufacturing it, there are three types of insulin, and each acts differently in the body:

- *Rapid- or regular-acting insulin:* This type of insulin reaches the bloodstream and begins lowering blood sugar within thirty minutes after it is injected, which is commonly known as "time of onset." Rapid- or regular-acting insulin reaches its maximum strength, or "peaks," about two to five hours later. It remains in the bloodstream for an additional eight to sixteen hours. This type of insulin is often used when a person's diabetes goes out of control, such as after hormonal shifts, changes in diet or exercise, an accident, minor surgery, or an illness.

- *Intermediate-acting insulin:* There are two types of intermediate-acting insulin: Lente (called L) and NPH (called N). These intermediate- or slow-acting insulins reach the bloodstream about ninety minutes after injection and peak anywhere between four and twelve hours later. They remain in the bloodstream for about twenty-four hours.

- *Long-acting insulin or Ultralente (called U):* Long-acting insulin usually takes about four to six hours to reach the bloodstream, but its effects last for about thirty-six hours. It tends to reach its maximum strength about fourteen to twenty-four hours after it has been injected.

Often, people will require a combination of different types of insulin, depending on their individual needs, eating habits, activity schedules, and particular course of disease.

Injecting Insulin

"At first," recalls Abigail, "getting shots three times a day was the worst part of having diabetes. I was only four and needles really scared me. Now that I'm older, I'm pretty used to it. But it still feels weird sometimes, and I know my friends are curious about it."

Most people consider daily injections to be one of the most daunting aspects of diabetes treatment—at least at first. Bonnie describes how she gives herself her daily injections: "First, I swab the area I will inject with alcohol to sterilize it. Then I open up a new needle and syringe and take up insulin from a bottle. I kind of bunch up the skin between my thumb and forefinger and, holding the needle at a right angle, I inject myself. I rotate where on my body I inject; sometimes it's in my upper arm, sometimes my abdomen, sometimes my thighs. When I was a kid and my parents injected me, they injected my buttocks."

Scientists have developed some new methods of injection that make the daily ritual of taking insulin less complicated:

- *Jet injectors:* This type of injector has no needle but instead delivers a tiny stream of insulin directly into the skin through a pressurized jet.

- *Insulin pens:* The insulin pen is a self-contained unit, with the needle and hormone in one container. As its name implies, this container looks like a pen and is just as easy to carry around.

- *Insulin pumps:* This device delivers a slow, time-released trickle of insulin into a person's body. Often worn on a waist belt, the pump feeds insulin from a storage vial through a plastic tube into a needle placed in the patient's abdomen or thigh. An insulin pump usually requires constant monitoring by both patient and doctor and therefore is used mostly by people in need of intensive therapy.

Maintaining Insulin Levels

Every person with diabetes has different needs for insulin, depending on daily activity levels and how his or her body responds to the hormone. Insulin is measured in units of cubic centimeters (cc), which are printed on the sides of syringes. Insulin is measured in three different strengths: 40, 80, and 100 units. Most people use the 100-unit concentration on a day-to-day basis.

Nora describes her typical daily dosage schedule: "I take a long-acting and a short-acting insulin. I take them both in one shot, and the long acting peaks in the middle of the night. Depending on what I eat and when I eat it, this combination seems to keep my blood sugar on an even keel most of the time."

There are some potential long-term complications of diabetes, as described in Chapter 1. But every day, a person with diabetes is at risk of suffering the less severe but just as frustrating side effects of poor insulin-level control.

When a person's blood sugar is too low—which may occur when too much insulin is taken or not enough food is eaten—a condition known as hypoglycemia may result. Hypoglycemia may cause irritability, dizziness, disorientation, weakness, exhaustion, and excessive sweating. If left untreated, this episode of low blood sugar (also known as an insulin reaction) could cause the diabetic to go into a coma. Twelve-year-old Mark describes how an insulin reaction feels to him: "For me, when I'm low, it feels like there's an earthquake going on inside my body."

When a person's blood sugar is too high—which may occur when not enough insulin is taken or when too much food is consumed—a condition known as hyperglycemia may result. A person with high blood sugar often experiences a very dry mouth and becomes very thirsty. He or she may urinate excessively and may feel unusually weak and irritable. If left untreated, hyperglycemia may lead to ketoacidosis and a diabetic coma.

Can people with diabetes feel themselves getting "high" or "low"? Most say that they can, and they know what to do to help themselves. When blood sugar is too low, they can usually solve the problem by drinking some orange juice or eating a few crackers. When blood sugar is too high, they can take some extra insulin or skip eating a scheduled meal.

Obviously, insulin alone does not solve the chemical imbalance known as diabetes. Instead, diet and amounts of exercise, sleep, and stress levels must be carefully regulated in order for good health to be maintained.

Maintaining Glucose Levels

People who have Type I diabetes must carefully monitor their blood-sugar (glucose) levels. Outside factors, such as emotional upsets, infection, hormonal changes, and alcohol and other drugs, may upset the necessary balance. Without monitoring glucose levels on a regular basis, the individual will not know if there's a problem until physical symptoms develop.

Fortunately, there are two types of home test kits. The first type, a urine test, measures the amount of glucose that has "spilled over" from the blood into the urine. Although urine testing is easy, it is not nearly as accurate as the second type of test, which is a blood test.

GLUCOSE IS A SIMPLE SUGAR THAT COMES FROM FOOD. IT IS THE FUEL THAT THE BODY'S CELLS USE FIRST AND IS THE BODY'S MAIN SOURCE OF ENERGY.

GLYCOGEN IS THE STORED FORM OF GLUCOSE. IT IS STORED IN THE LIVER AND MUSCLES UNTIL IT IS NEEDED, THEN IS CONVERTED INTO GLUCOSE AND RELEASED INTO THE BLOODSTREAM.

Blood tests for glucose also come in kits, complete with testing instructions and materials. The person testing his or her blood pricks one fingertip with a device called a lancer, which is designed to draw a single drop of blood. The blood is placed on a chemically treated strip and, depending on the type of strip used, the blood is blotted after thirty, sixty, or ninety seconds. In some kits, the strip of paper changes color according to how much glucose is present in the blood. Other kits contain a mechanical meter that automatically displays the blood-glucose level.

Finding a Balance

Learning to balance diet, exercise, and insulin requirements is one of the great challenges that face each individual with diabetes. It is not a balance that can usually be established during the first weeks or even the first months of living with the illness. Instead it may take many months or even years to establish. Our bodies are constantly changing as we grow older and as we change our habits, and so the challenge of controlling and regulating diabetes care is an ongoing, lifelong process. Even people who have had diabetes for several years often have to adjust their schedules and dosages according to how their bodies are responding to both internal and external factors.

In Chapter 3, Bonnie, Rachel, and some of their peers will describe how they established healthy routines based on their individual lifestyles and body chemistries.

Chapter Three

THE BALANCING ACT

Most people grab a snack whenever they feel like it. They may decide to play a game of tennis or basketball on the spur of the moment. Such spontaneity, however, may be dangerous for people with diabetes, who must plan carefully and well in advance what to eat and how much to exercise. In fact, planning and sticking to an eating and exercise schedule are often harder than taking insulin on a daily basis. As Bonnie says: "I thought getting the shots was the worst part about diabetes, but it isn't half as bad as trying to figure out what to eat every meal. Sometimes I just want to eat what I want to eat."

DIET AND NUTRITION

People with Type I diabetes must pay particular attention to when they eat and how much they eat to ensure that the insulin they inject will metabolize their food properly. Although their daily meal plans may be a bit complicated, and sometimes quite rigid, they follow the same general rules of nutrition as people without diabetes.

A well-balanced diet is essential for people with diabetes. Complex carbohydrates, found in grains, fruits, and vegetables, are particularly important because they are digested slowly.

Bonnie is hardly alone in her desire to break away from nutritional rules and regulations and just eat what she wants. But everyone—with or without diabetes—must eat good food in the right amounts in order to stay healthy. To maintain our health, we all must learn what our bodies need to survive and then satisfy those needs with the food we eat.

A healthy diet for a person with diabetes is not very different from that of a person without the disease. The human laboratory requires about forty different essential nutrients in order to carry out bodily functions and maintain the body's health. There are six different types of food—carbohydrates, fruits, vegetables, dairy, protein, and fats—that we need to eat in order to obtain all of the nutrients our bodies require.

- *Carbohydrates:* Carbohydrates are the body's major source of energy. Once digested, they are broken down and either used as fuel, called glucose, by the cells or stored in the liver or muscles as glycogen for later use. In the process of photosynthesis, green plants form carbohydrates from carbon dioxide and water as they convert sunlight into energy. All plant material, including grains, fruits, and vegetables contain some carbohydrates.

  Complex carbohydrates, also known as starches, are of special importance. Breads, cereals, grains, pasta, fruits, and vegetables are all complex carbohydrates. Foods composed of complex carbohydrates are generally low in fat, high in fiber, and have a lot of nutritional extras. A slice of whole-wheat bread, for instance, contains not only carbohydrates but also protein, fiber, and several other nutrients, including riboflavin, thiamine, calcium, and iron. Simple carbohydrates, on the other hand, consist mainly of sugar. Simple carbohydrates are found in high-calorie, high-fat items, like cookies and cake.

  According to most nutritionists, we all should strive to consume fewer simple carbohydrates and more complex carbohydrates—about 50 to 60 percent of our daily calories should come from whole grains, pasta, fruits, and vegetables. For people with diabetes, these guidelines are especially important. Simple carbohydrates are digested very quickly and broken down into glucose, which rapidly raises blood-sugar levels. Complex carbohydrates, on the other hand, take longer to digest and thus enter the bloodstream more slowly.

CARBOHYDRATES ARE PRODUCED NATURALLY BY GREEN PLANTS FROM CARBON DIOXIDE AND WATER. THEY SUPPLY GLUCOSE, THE PRIMARY SOURCE OF ENERGY FOR THE BODY, AND ARE UTILIZED IN THE PRODUCTION OF FATS. MOST GLUCOSE IS DERIVED FROM THE CARBOHYDRATES FOUND IN GRAINS, CEREALS, PASTA, POTATOES, BEANS, AND SEVERAL DIFFERENT KINDS OF FRUITS AND VEGETABLES.

• *Fruits and vegetables:* With few exceptions, all fruits and vegetables are low in fat and calories, high in fiber, and full of vitamins and minerals. In fact, fruits and vegetables provide about 90 percent of the vitamin C and half of the vitamin A in the nation's food supply, while contributing just 9 percent of the calories. Fruits and vegetables are healthful and preparation-free snack foods for everyone, particularly for people with diabetes.

• *Protein:* The term protein comes from the Greek word *protos*, which means "first and foremost." Indeed, proteins are found in every body cell, compose the second most plentiful substance (after water) in the body, and constitute about one-fifth of body weight. Protein is the major component of our muscles, organs, bones, skin, immune-system cells, some hormones, and virtually all enzymes (substances that speed up the rate of biochemical actions).

Proteins are made up of organic compounds called amino acids. There are twenty-two amino acids. Of these, the body can manufacture all but ten. These ten are called "essential amino acids" and must be obtained from the food we eat. Meat, fish, egg whites, milk, and other animal products are the best sources of dietary protein. Plant material, specifically grains, legumes (beans and peas), and certain vegetables also contain varying amounts of proteins. Soybean products are also a good source of protein.

We need very little protein to maintain our health: about 5 to 8 ounces (142 to 227 grams) of meat over the course of a day provides teenagers—with and without diabetes—with all the protein they need to build strong bones and muscles. Adults require even less, about 3 to 4 ounces (85 to 113 grams) per day or about 12 to 20 percent of daily calories. What's especially important for those with diabetes is the source of the protein: Some animal products, like cheese and beef, tend to be also very high in fat and calories. Fish, legumes, and lean meats, on the other hand, are more healthful choices.

• *Dairy products:* Foods like cheese, milk, and yogurt are rich in several important nutrients, including calcium. Calcium is an essential ingredient in the formation of bones and teeth. Most young adults—with and without diabetes—need to consume about 12 ounces (340 grams) of dairy products every day to meet their nutritional requirements.

• *Fat:* Every day, we hear warnings about the dangers of eating too much fat. Too much fat in the body contributes to a host of health problems, including heart disease, high blood pressure, certain types of cancer, and obesity. Type II diabetes, which develops mostly in people age forty and older, is directly related to obesity and too much fat in the diet. Although we should all limit the amount of fat we eat, we should not eliminate it completely from our diets. Everyone needs to consume some fat daily, although groups and individuals differ in their opinions about how much fat we should consume to be healthy. According to the Food and Drug Administration, less than 30 percent of our daily calories should come from fat; others believe that fat should make up 10 percent or less of our daily calories.

In addition to the major food groups, people with diabetes have to pay special attention to the amount of the following substances that are included in the daily eating plan:

• *Sugar:* People with Type I diabetes should avoid eating candy, cake, pastries, sodas, and other foods high in processed sugar, which may cause blood-sugar levels to rise to dangerous levels. Fortunately, several sugar substitutes, such as sorbitol, aspartame, and saccharin, are available to satisfy a sweet tooth—although they may have other health risks and should be used in moderation. Many foods that contain natural sugar, such as fruits and fruit juice, are healthy choices for people with diabetes.

• *Salt:* People with diabetes should generally avoid foods that have a lot of salt in them. Salt often affects the circulatory system, the system that delivers blood to body organs and tissues, by raising the blood pressure. Herbs and low-salt spices can be used to flavor foods instead.

Snacking is as much a part of the life of an American teenager as television and soccer games, but for people with diabetes it poses some special challenges. Cookies, candy, and chips are generally off-limits for people with diabetes, and so is overeating or eating at unscheduled times. The goal of treatment is to keep glucose levels stable throughout the day, so eating small amounts of healthy foods, like dried fruit, cheese, and nuts, several times a day is often recommended. Ten-year-old Abigail says: "My friends at school think I'm so lucky because I get to eat snacks all the time, but really I would rather not have diabetes than have a few extra treats during the day."

No food is ever completely off-limits for a person with diabetes; as long as it's planned for, an occasional piece of chocolate cake or a handful or two of potato chips can be enjoyed. "At first, I was nervous about going to birthday parties because I didn't want to look like a geek who couldn't eat anything but carrot sticks," admits Abigail. "But pretty soon, I had a pretty good system worked out. I could have a small piece of cake if I knew we'd be doing a lot of activity afterwards—like playing tag or something—to burn off the extra sugar. And, with the help of a nutritionist, I chose some yummy snacks to bring along, like fruit roll-ups and stuff, that everyone wanted to share."

CREATING A MEAL PLAN

For people with diabetes, adhering to a strict diet means planning their days as best they can in advance, and sometimes sacrificing a certain amount of freedom and spontaneity. Nutritionists can help people plan daily eating schedules and menus that best suit individual needs, wants, and habits, allowing some room for flexibility. Nutritionists also are able to recommend helpful cookbooks and other resources so that patients and families can take advantage of the many food options available without compromising health. With time, effort, and advice from a nutritionist, most young people find that they have plenty of healthful and delicious food choices.

The key to living well with diabetes is following a consistent, balanced meal plan, one that includes the right amount of nutrients and schedules foods to be eaten at the right times.

The following sample menu plan shows you the kinds of foods that young adults with diabetes might eat on any given day—it isn't much different than what those without the disorder might also choose.

Following a meal plan does not have to interfere with parties or other social activities. It's best to have healthy snacks, but no type of food is completely off-limits, as long as it's been included in the meal plan.

SAMPLE MEAL PLAN

Breakfast: half glass of orange juice
two slices of toast
unsweetened cereal with 1 cup
    (250 milliliters) of whole milk

Snack: two whole-wheat crackers and cheese

Lunch: turkey and cheese sandwich
vegetable soup
carrot sticks
apple

Snack: piece of fruit, handful of nuts

Dinner: 4 to 5 ounces (113–142 grams) of
    chicken or fish
string beans
baked potato
salad
banana, sugar-free cookie

There are bound to be times when adhering to a meal plan is not possible. People with diabetes should understand that such "slips" in routine are common, and can usually be managed without causing any long-term ill effects. In fact, feeling guilty and out-of-control because of a few mistakes or indulgences may be upsetting to blood-sugar levels and general health. It's best simply to compensate by adding insulin or extra food and then start over again with good planning and adherence the next day.

In general, there are three basic nutritional principles that young people with diabetes should try to follow as best they can:

1. Be as consistent with meal times, portions, and variety of foods as possible.
2. Eat some extra food before engaging in more physical activity than normal.
3. Inject extra insulin if extra food is eaten during the day.

It's important for people with diabetes to recognize when their blood-sugar levels are becoming too high or too low. Nora explains:

> It's especially tricky to realize that your blood sugar is too high and you have to eat dinner anyway—like if you're going to a play or something. What I do is take extra insulin and hope that my blood sugar comes down. It's a bit of risk, but I usually find that the extra insulin doesn't cause a problem. If it does, I try to eat a little less starch. It's one big balancing act between not letting glucose levels get too high and then not letting them dip too low.

As Nora is starting to learn, people who have diabetes usually know their bodies well enough to plan for exceptions and interruptions in their daily schedules, especially when extra physical activity is involved.

GETTING ENOUGH EXERCISE

One out of every three people in the United States is overweight. There are two main reasons for this alarmingly high statistic: We eat too many calories and too much fat every day, and we do not get enough exercise.

Very few Americans—young or old—engage in enough physical activity to keep their bodies healthy and fit. Physical activity tones muscles, keeps internal organs (including the heart), in good working order, relieves stress, and improves a person's mood. Running, jumping, swimming, biking, and other forms of aerobic exercise make us feel better by releasing specific hormones as well as by providing an outlet for anger, frustration, and aggression.

For people with diabetes, exercise is especially important for several reasons. The amount of exercise a person gets each day affects the body's insulin level, just as the amount of food a person eats and when it is eaten affects it. If someone's blood sugar is too high, exercise is one of the best methods of restoring it to a normal level.

THE TERM AEROBIC REFERS TO THE USE OF OXYGEN. CERTAIN TYPES OF VIGOROUS EXERCISE, LIKE RUNNING, BIKING, SWIMMING, AND SKIING, ARE PARTICULARLY BENEFICIAL BECAUSE THEY REQUIRE YOUR BODY TO USE OXYGEN MORE EFFICIENTLY. YOUR MUSCLES BECOME STRONGER, YOUR CELLS ARE BATHED IN OXYGEN AND OTHER NUTRIENTS, AND YOUR INTERNAL ORGANS WORK AT OPTIMUM CAPACITY.

Also, when people with diabetes exercise, they need less insulin because the physical activity increases the body's sensitivity to insulin and helps the body burn glucose more efficiently. Another advantage to exercising regularly is that, because activity burns calories very efficiently, it's possible to eat more food without gaining weight—a definite plus for everyone, with or without diabetes.

Although almost all young people with diabetes can play any kind of sport, they need to keep a careful eye on the way that exercise affects their blood-sugar levels. Blood sugars can fluctuate quickly, and it is not uncommon for people with diabetes to suffer from an attack of hypoglycemia (low blood sugar) during strenuous exercise. As described in Chapter 2, symptoms of hypoglycemia include excessive sweating, disorientation, and exhaustion. Because of this common side effect, doctors recommend that people with diabetes carry sugar tablets or containers of fruit juice to consume if blood-sugar levels begin to plummet. In addition, young people with diabetes should let teachers, athletic coaches, and their playmates and teammates know of their condition in case they need assistance during activity.

Most medical professionals recommend a thirty-minute workout about four times a week. Each workout should get the heart pumping, the muscles working, and the body sweating. For those with diabetes, it's important to keep the following suggestions in mind:

- Exercise at the same time every day. This will also help you maintain a regular schedule of meals and insulin injections.

- Exercise an hour after mealtime to lower glucose levels just when they are at their highest.

- Test blood-sugar levels before exercising in order to avoid hypoglycemia.

- Try to eat a snack about fifteen to twenty minutes before exercising in order to provide the body with the extra glucose it will need to perform the extra activity.

- Choose an activity you enjoy. Exercise should be fun and feel good. If you are not enjoying one activity, try another.

A lot of planning goes into the day of a person with diabetes. As Nora points out, however, it is important not to let the pressure of planning take over every moment. This pressure is often more than young adults can handle by themselves. Sometimes, the stresses and strains of coping with diabetes interfere with relationships, self-esteem, and other challenging parts of a young person's life.

51

Chapter Four

THE CHALLENGES OF ADOLESCENCE

During adolescence, many physical, emotional, and social changes take place. Having diabetes adds yet another set of pressures to the already stressful existence of many young people. Nora recalls: "I think it was much harder for me to be diagnosed with diabetes when I was just starting adolescence. If I'd been diagnosed as a little kid, I would have had years to get used to it before all the changes of adolescence hit me."

Traditionally, during the teen years, adolescents begin to separate from their parents, rebel against authority, and establish their own sense of themselves and their place in the world. By the time most young people enter junior high or high school, they have begun to take more responsibility for their own lives. They're choosing what to wear, what music they like to listen to, what kind of friends they enjoy hanging out with. Most start dating, learn to drive a car, and even start to think about long-term plans, such as marriage and careers.

During this period, young people are also passing through some of the most dramatic physical changes of

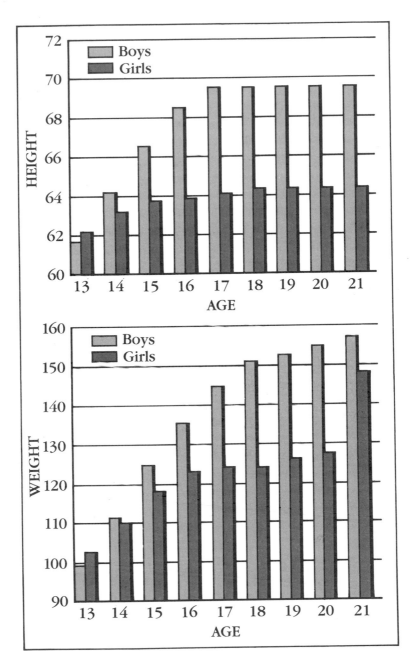

Typical changes in height and weight in adolescents.

DURING THE FIRST EIGHTEEN TO TWENTY YEARS OF LIFE, MOST PEOPLE EXPERIENCE OCCASIONAL AND SUDDEN PERIODS OF PHYSICAL GROWTH. THE PERIOD OF ADOLESCENCE IS A PARTICULARLY ACTIVE PHASE OF THE MATURATION PROCESS, BECAUSE GROWTH AND SEX HORMONES ARE BEING PRODUCED IN GREAT QUANTITIES AT THIS TIME.

their lives. The adolescent body grows at a more rapid rate than at any other time of life except infancy. Body weight almost doubles, and height increases by approximately 25 percent. Coping with all of these physical and emotional changes, while at the same time learning to manage a chronic illness like diabetes, poses a remarkable challenge to young adults.

THE PHYSICAL CHANGES

One of the most frustrating aspects of having diabetes during one's adolescence is that management and control of one's blood sugar become more difficult. A person could be very careful about diet and exercise, yet for seemingly no reason at all, his or her blood-sugar levels go out of control. One reason for such fluctuations is the surge in hormone levels that occurs during this period of life. Growth hormone (GH), necessary for adolescent bone and muscle growth, also acts as an anti-insulin agent, preventing the hormone from breaking down glucose efficiently. In addition, male and female sex hormones—estrogen and testosterone—are also first produced during adolescence, provoking many emotional and physical changes.

These fundamental changes require an enormous amount of energy to be expended by the body's cells, which may cause sudden shifts in body chemistry and hormone levels. In someone with diabetes, such shifts can result in frequent—and frequently unpleasant—insulin reactions. As Nora comments: "The hardest times for me were the severe insulin reactions I had because my hormones were going crazy, which I think had a lot to do with being a teenager. I was taken to the emergency room a lot during high school."

One of the keys to maintaining good health during adolescence is establishing a good working relationship with your medical team—communicating openly and honestly with doctors, nurses, and other health professionals. Because fifteen-year-old Robert had a good relationship with his doctor, the doctor was able to recognize when Robert was having difficulty controlling his diabetes. "I was having all these mood swings, and I was tired all the time," recalls Robert. "My mom said I was just being a typical teenager, but my doctor could see that I was reacting badly to my insulin. She did that not only by doing medical tests, but by really listening to me when I described how I felt."

"I really appreciated the doctor who told me how serious my diabetes was," thirteen-year-old Susan admits. "It seemed like the second I turned twelve, everything went haywire. For four years, I'd been using the same dosages of insulin, at the same times every day. Then, all of a sudden, my blood sugar went out of control, swinging high and low without me doing anything different. My doctor said I had to be really careful, and helped me figure out what would work for me. I don't think I could have managed it without him."

THE STRUGGLE FOR INDEPENDENCE

People with diabetes must follow a number of rules in order to maintain good control and health. During adolescence, however, most young people—with and without chronic illnesses like diabetes—get tired of following rules set down by parents, teachers, doctors, and other authority figures. Young adults at this time strive to become independent, and for persons with diabetes, this often means deciding to take on more responsibility for their own care. Unfortunately, in some cases, this struggle for independence often translates into rebellion against all authority figures and their rules—including doctors and the rules they outline for maintaining control over diabetes. Many teenagers stop taking care of themselves—eating too much or too little, neglecting their insulin injection regimens, and doing too little or too much exercise—as a way of asserting their independence. Such lapses in care can have dangerous short-and long-term effects, as Katie now understands:

> *I realize that in the last two years I've been in a stubborn stage, and I haven't been taking care of myself. I'm starting to learn how stupid that is, because I'm starting to suffer some physical problems because of it. Still, though, I haven't gotten to the point where I'm able to take better care of myself. My blood sugar gets low, and for some reason I don't go get some juice. Maybe it's just that I don't want to deal with my diabetes.*

Like Katie, most teenagers will admit that while they consider becoming independent very important, they also have mixed feelings about growing up and coping with life on their own. Having diabetes only complicates these already ambivalent feelings because of the added responsibilities the disorder puts upon people who have it.

FITTING IN

Most teenagers feel as if the changes they're experiencing are only happening to them and not to anyone else. They feel different and alone but, at the same time, yearn to fit in with their peers, to be part of the crowd. Because they

Like other teenagers, young people with diabetes have concerns about fitting in with friends. Many fear being rejected because of their condition, but find instead that true friends will help and support them.

have poor images of themselves, many teenagers, whether they have diabetes or not, develop eating disorders, reckless habits, and addictive behavior. They desperately want to be perceived as "normal" and to dull the bad feelings they may have about themselves.

These feelings of isolation and low self-esteem are heightened for many teens with diabetes, who feel somehow abnormal, unlike their peers.

As Rachel says: "I just want to be like everybody else. I don't want my diabetes to make me different." Teens with diabetes must take regular shots of insulin, cannot indulge in junk-food binges, and must be constantly mindful of how much exercise they perform every day.

"It would depress me," says Nora, "I just felt that I couldn't be like everybody else. I would always feel different from my friends in that respect. And my friends never even knew I had diabetes."

ESTABLISHING AN IDENTITY

Figuring out "who I am" is the focus of many people during their teen years. The self-image that develops during this period is likely to be the one that is carried throughout one's life. Young people struggle to define their personalities and locate their places in the world around them. They make and revise plans for the future countless times. They continually explore, reject, and seek out new interests and hobbies. A teenager's social interactions with peers contribute to self-esteem and pave the way for healthy adult relationships.

Having a chronic illness like diabetes during adolescence also influences the shape and form of a teenager's personality and self-image. Whether or not this influence is positive or negative depends, at least in part, on how the teenager thinks others view the disease. If a teen with diabetes feels that friends and family accept the condition as a normal part of life, then he or she is more likely to accept it, too.

A common wish among teens with diabetes is that people—strangers and friends—would simply ask about the disease. Twelve-year-old Mark remembers when he had a slight insulin reaction while standing in a movie line. He was sweating and trembling for a few moments before the candy he ate rebalanced his blood sugar. "The people behind me were whispering and staring. I would have been glad to tell them what was going on if they'd asked, but they didn't. It made me feel pretty weird."

Everyone needs to be aware that the lives of people with diabetes are no less meaningful or rich with potential than the lives of people without the condition.

DATING

Feeling attractive to the opposite sex becomes extremely important during the teenage years. Having diabetes by no means prevents a teenager from dating casually, falling in love, or having dreams of marriage and children. It does, however, add a few challenges to the often difficult and awkward teenage dating process. While many teens have come to terms with their disorder in other arenas—with friends, family, even strangers—facing the opposite sex can be intimidating. "No one can tell that I have diabetes just by looking at me," fifteen-year-old Katie says. "In fact, I've had several dates with guys who never knew. But it's one more thing that I'm nervous about."

The careful planning and coordination of meals and activities that are a necessary part of diabetes control may disrupt a normal dating pattern. One girl that Robert dated, for instance, was so annoyed by his need for schedules that she broke up with him after just a few weeks. "To be truthful, I'm not sure it was the diabetes itself," Robert says. "I think I'm just normally a pretty staid sort of person, while she was kind of a spur-of-the-moment type."

Robert realizes that his preference for planning and keeping to a schedule is as much a part of his personality as it is a necessary part of his treatment. Not everyone, however, is as objective as Robert, but it is important for teens with diabetes to distinguish between those aspects of their relationships that are influenced by their condition and those that are simply expressions of their own or others' personalities.

DRUGS, ALCOHOL, AND EATING DISORDERS

Adolescence is often a time for experimentation with new and forbidden substances and behaviors. Some young people try to fit in with their peer group by taking drugs and alcohol. Drinking and taking drugs have many inherent risks, but for those with diabetes, these risks are multiplied substantially. Both alcohol and drugs affect metabolism (the rate at which the body uses energy) and make it almost impossible for a person with diabetes to control blood-sugar levels. Chemical substances also impair judgment, which means that people with diabetes are less likely to be aware of the changes occurring in their bodies and thus unable to take proper precautions when necessary.

While taking drugs and drinking alcohol may seem like fun to some teens, many find such potentially dangerous behavior frightening. As Katie says: "The idea that you could go out to a club and possibly get drunk, or that you could smoke a joint, is scary. I'm not planning to go out and do that, but if I were to get drunk, I know I would never be able to control my diabetes; I'd never know if my blood sugar was too high or low. And that's scary."

If a teenager with diabetes knows the risks but decides to drink anyway, he or she should also be aware of the effects that behavior could have. "Luckily, it's okay not to drink at my school. I mean, you don't feel left out if you refuse," Robert says. "But I'd be lying if I said I haven't had a beer to feel part of a group at a party or something. But I stop at one, then drink club soda. I always carry extra insulin in case I overdo it, and my good friends know what to do if something goes wrong."

Another common and risky behavior, especially for those with diabetes, is extreme dieting. Many young women go on crash diets and nearly starve themselves to achieve a certain body type deemed popular by their peers. For those with diabetes, however, crash dieting can cause sudden changes in insulin and blood-sugar levels, resulting in both hypo- and hyperglycemia.

Anorexia nervosa is one of two common eating disorders among teens. A person suffering from anorexia nervosa has an intense fear of eating and gaining weight and actually refuses to take food, often to the point of starving. Bulimia is a condition in which a person has regular episodes of binge eating followed by forced vomiting.

Nora tells how she struggled with anorexia:

> I felt overweight all my life. During high school, I wanted to lose ten pounds, but because I was diabetic, I thought I couldn't. How could I diet if I didn't skip meals?
>
> I think I had all the symptoms of a potential eating disorder: I hated the way I looked in clothes. I thought I was fat. I couldn't stand my body. When I started to lose weight, I remember thinking, "I can do this." I became completely neurotic about what I ate. I had an obsession with numbers: how much did I weigh, what was my blood sugar, how many calories were in an apple. The whole thing—being diabetic and anorexic— fed into each other.
>
> If I discovered that my blood sugar was high, I would just get hysterical. When it was low, I

*would eat a lot of sugar tablets and became addict-
ed to them. I thought if I could eat the tablets,
drink one cup of coffee, and eat a few spears of
asparagus, that was a good day of eating.*

ANOREXIA NERVOSA AND BULIMIA ARE EATING
DISORDERS THAT MOST COMMONLY AFFECT
TEENAGE GIRLS AND, OCCASIONALLY, TEENAGE
BOYS. THESE YOUNG ADULTS OFTEN FEEL INADE-
QUATE, DEPRESSED, AND NERVOUS ABOUT
GROWING UP.

PEOPLE WITH ANOREXIA HAVE AN INTENSE
FEAR OF FOOD AND OF GAINING WEIGHT, AND
OFTEN REFUSE TO EAT ANYTHING AT ALL. THOSE
WITH BULIMIA GENERALLY BINGE—EAT TREMEN-
DOUS AMOUNTS OF FOOD—THEN FORCE THEM-
SELVES TO VOMIT. PEOPLE WITH EITHER OF THESE
EATING DISORDERS USUALLY HAVE A DISTORTED
BODY IMAGE AND EXTREMELY LOW SELF-ESTEEM.

After playing this dangerous game for almost a year,
Nora's eyesight began to get blurry, and she saw flashes of
light. Her doctor diagnosed retinopathy—a disease in
which the blood vessels in the eyes become damaged—and
attempted to correct it with laser surgery. Fortunately, the
operation was a success and her eyesight was saved.

*It's because I'm diabetic that the eating disorder
was caught so early. I was walking around with
low blood sugar so much that it was affecting my
state of mind. I don't know how I managed to fin-
ish school that year. I think I was lucky that I was
diagnosed and then hospitalized when I was. The
doctors told me that I would have been almost
blind within a year—maybe even dead—if I had
kept going at that rate.*

Melisssa Strugger is a social worker who helps young people cope with diabetes. She says: "People with diabetes don't have to vomit to purge. Instead, they simply don't take their insulin. What happens is that as blood-sugar levels run high, the excess glucose—along with all the excess calories—is excreted through urine. It's a very dangerous thing to do, and can lead to all kinds of problems."

Eating disorders often go unnoticed for some time, and by the time they are noticed in people with diabetes, the patients usually have to be hospitalized in order to stabilize their conditions. Once the physical problems have been resolved, psychological counseling takes place on an ongoing basis in order to address the underlying self-esteem and body issues.

So many changes occur in a person's life during adolescence that it's hard to make sense of them all. And, unfortunately, the extra care and attention that diabetes requires of a young adult only compound the difficulty of coping with these many new challenges. In the next chapter, we will hear how some young adults with diabetes have learned to live in a world in which most people do not share the same daily health concerns.

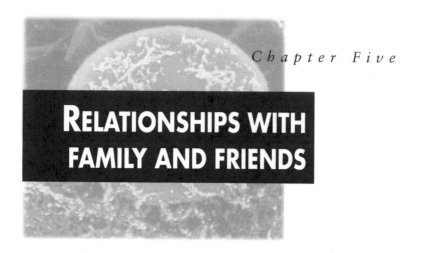

Chapter Five

RELATIONSHIPS WITH FAMILY AND FRIENDS

During adolescence, family relationships begin to change, sometimes dramatically, whether a chronic illness like diabetes is a factor or not. Breaking away from parents—a natural process that starts in early childhood—is made more difficult for a young person when the parents' support and knowledge are needed to help manage the day-to-day care connected with diabetes. Relationships between sisters and brothers also sometimes become strained as rivalries intensify and personalities become more defined. Working through these changes and adjustments becomes another challenge—an exciting and often rewarding one—for the person with diabetes.

GETTING ALONG WITH PARENTS

"I wouldn't be able to deal with diabetes at all if it wasn't for my parents." This was the almost unanimous refrain from the young people interviewed for this book. Fourteen-year-old Bonnie claims that in the eight years since her diagnosis, she and her parents have become closer than ever. "My folks never left my side when I was in the hospital when I was six, and they've been right there with me all along. I know I couldn't have made it without them."

Most teens are sincerely grateful for their parents' support. Many also wish that there were limits to their parents' involvement in their everyday activities. These mixed feelings are perfectly normal. When an adolescent is diagnosed with diabetes, the care and concern of parents are even harder to cope with because, during this period of life, the child wants more freedom and independence.

Although twelve-year-old Mark knows that his mother has his best interests at heart, he feels that she is sometimes overprotective.

> *Every time I leave the house, my mother asks if I have a piece of fruit or candy with me in case my blood sugar goes low, extra insulin in case it goes high, my doctor's phone number, everything. She even makes me take a couple extra quarters so that I can make a phone call if I'm feeling sick and want her to pick me up. And she usually manages to say all this stuff in front of my friends, so I feel like a baby.*

In the minds of most teens, there's a fine line between caring and nagging. If parents are constantly nagging, however, the normal rebellious feelings may be much harder to suppress.

Guilt plagues both children with diabetes and their parents—the children feel guilty about all the extra stress and strain their illness puts on the family, and parents often secretly and mistakenly believe that they are somehow responsible for their child's illness.

Sometimes a parent expresses guilt by denying the seriousness of the condition, as was true for the father of eleven-year-old Rachel. For about a year after her diagnosis, Rachel's father downplayed the havoc the disease was creating in Rachel's life. "He'd say things like 'Oh, you can

With open and honest communication, parents and children can work together to manage the practical and emotional aspects of living with diabetes.

eat this extra piece of cake, you're a growing girl,' when eating at that time would screw up my blood sugar. I know he wasn't trying to be mean or careless, he just wanted to make me feel normal."

. Children are sometimes very angry with their parents and blame the parents for giving them the illness. They are also upset when their parents insist that they take shots, stick to meal plans, and perform a regular regimen of daily exercise. Sometimes, the hidden feelings of anger and guilt are expressed in other ways, leading to confusion and mis-understandings. "I remember a time when my parents were planning a family vacation that had to be changed because I had an important doctor's appointment," Katie recalls. "I threw a fit—screaming and crying—and my parents thought that I was upset because I couldn't go. So they felt really bad for me. But I wasn't upset because I couldn't go, I was upset because they couldn't go. We were both feeling guilty and sad, but for the wrong reasons."

Finding the right balance between overprotectiveness and support, authority and independence, and control and trust is difficult for any parent and for any child. Open and honest communication is the key, especially for families who face the challenges of diabetes. Bonnie feels that because her parents were always open and positive about her diabetes, she is at ease with her condition and with her care. Her parents' attitude has also made it easier for Bonnie to be open with her friends about her illness.

SIBLING RIVALRY

Parents are not the only people who have to make adjustments when a member of the family is diagnosed with diabetes. Brothers and sisters must also face the challenges presented by having a sibling with a chronic illness. Although they are friends, competitors, sometimes even full-fledged enemies, siblings have uniquely close, intimate relationships. Relationships between siblings can form some of the strongest, most enduring bonds in a person's life. Brothers and sisters help to shape one another's lives and prepare for experiences with peers and as adults. Chronic illness like diabetes often adds special meaning to these close bonds.

"I guess it happens a lot, but once when my older sister was mad, she wished something terrible would happen to me," Bonnie remembers. "A few days later, I was diagnosed with diabetes. I think that even now, eight years later, she still feels a little guilty, even though she knows she had nothing to do with it."

Bonnie is right: Guilt about a chronic illness in the family affects siblings almost as much as it affects parents. Brothers and sister, especially when they are young, often bear the burden of responsibility for their ill sibling's condition.

Feelings of guilt can arise from, or be intensified by, a poor understanding of what diabetes is. In an effort to shield them, parents often do not share accurate information with the other children in the family. The siblings then interpret for themselves all that is seen, heard, and sensed. These often-distorted interpretations may be more frightening than the truth.

Along with guilt and fear, siblings often feel resentment: resentment over the extra attention paid to the child with diabetes by parents, other relatives, and friends; resentment over disruptions in family routines. Many parents find it difficult to divide their attention and support equally between a healthy child and a child with an illness. The healthy child's needs often take second place to the ongoing and sometimes urgent challenge of coping with a chronic illness like diabetes.

But the child with diabetes can feel resentment, too, for special treatment given to his or her siblings. Although he jokes about it now, Robert, who is now fifteen, remembers that his father treated him differently from his brother. "My brother's almost nine years younger than I am, so I don't really mind, but he does get to do things I wasn't allowed to do, like go to sleepovers and go camping. It

Siblings also often have to make adjustments when a brother or sister has diabetes.

wasn't until last year that I could be away from home for more than twenty-four hours."

Some siblings, however, like Rachel's sister Mandy, are understanding from the start. Mandy chooses not to eat foods that her older sister is unable to eat—at least not in front of her. Instead, she indulgences in sweet treats on the afternoons she spends alone with her mother, who takes special care to give Mandy extra attention.

As is true for parents, siblings often need a period of adjustment after someone in the family is diagnosed with diabetes. As time passes and life resumes a more normal pace and tone, most brothers and sisters reestablish their former relationships with each other. Sometimes, coping with diabetes together helps them form even deeper connections. Indeed, despite all the conflict, most young people with diabetes wouldn't trade their siblings for anything. "My brother's a pest sometimes," admits Robert, "but I can't imagine what it would be like without him."

RELATIONSHIPS WITH FRIENDS

Forming relationships with people their own age helps young people define their personalities. Experimenting with all aspects of behavior and image—from style of dress to musical tastes and political ideals—is a natural part of the process of becoming an adult.

At the same time, however, conforming to the tastes and standards of the majority is equally important, especially as young people enter adolescence. "Fitting in" is a crucial aspect of personal growth for teenagers, who fear that deviating from the mainstream might result in being labeled a "nerd" or something worse. Having a chronic illness makes the young people who have it slightly "different." Taking medication, eating a special diet, experiencing visible symptoms such as insulin reactions—all of these aspects of chronic illness interfere with a young person's efforts to fit in with his or her peer group and frequently result in teasing and exclusion.

Friends of those with diabetes should realize that although their friends may not look or act any differently, they might feel uncomfortable when special attention is drawn to them or when people have the wrong idea about what diabetes is.

Ten-year-old Abigail confides that "some of my friends think I'm lucky because I get special attention, but a couple of my close friends really understand how difficult diabetes can really be for me." It is comforting to young people with diabetes to know that there are people who realize that what they have to do is not fun. Abigail wants her friends to know that when she was diagnosed with diabetes, she felt as if her childhood was taken from her. "I know I'm still only ten, but I feel much older," she admits. "Diabetes doesn't let you be a kid. You grow up as soon as you get it."

Many young people feel that if they tell their friends about their diabetes, they will be excluded from parties and other social activities. Nora says: "I was sure that if too many people knew I had diabetes, I would never be invited to another person's house again. I did not want to take the chance of being rejected by my friends."

Nora learned, after having several severe insulin reactions as a teenager, that it would be safer to tell people about her condition. She also feels that "it's really important for people with diabetes to know that their illness is not the most significant thing about them to their friends. My friends know that I'm a great cook and that I love to ski—and my disease doesn't get in the way of my enjoyment of eating or physical activity."

The most prevalent fear among young people with diabetes is that their peers will reject them if they discover that they have the disease. More often than not, however, this is not the case. In fact, most young people find that their true friends are eager to learn about the disease and about what they can do to help make coping with it just a little bit easier—especially at school where the challenges are many.

AT SCHOOL

All of the aspects of diabetes care—taking medication, coping with sugar highs and lows, snacking between meals, testing glucose levels—tend to interfere with a normal school day. Rachel, who has a busy schedule of classes and sports at school, says: "I don't want to leave a class to deal with my diabetes, but I know if I feel like my blood sugar is going low that I have to get some juice. So I just do it." Rachel also knows that her friends understand why she sometimes has to leave in the middle of a discussion or lecture. Both she and her parents have talked to her friends and their parents, which dispelled much of the mystery about Rachel's condition.

Sometimes, though, going to school can be a frightening experience, especially immediately after the diagnosis, as it was for Nora. "Going back to school was difficult. The night before I went back to school, my best friend called and said she was so nervous around me she didn't know what to say. That really depressed me because I thought I hadn't changed at all, that there was nothing different about me."

Because of her friend's reaction, Nora told very few people at school about her illness, and now, many years later, she wishes that she had felt comfortable enough to share more. She knows it is much safer for friends and teachers to know about diabetes than it is to keep it a secret. Bonnie learned this lesson early. "I've told all my friends because I feel much more secure when everyone knows. I don't have a problem telling people I have diabetes because it's not like it's a contagious disease or anything. And then if I get into trouble or anything, they'll all know what to do."

Mark also thinks it's smart for people to know. "Most people are curious about it, and I don't mind telling them. In fact, I'm glad that they're interested in me."

Abigail decided to tell her class about diabetes and brought all her equipment into school to show her peers and teachers what she has to do each day. Susan also gave a presentation to her class after she was first diagnosed, which helped her friends and classmates better understand her condition.

Apart from the social challenges involved in going to school, those with chronic illnesses face other hurdles in the academic atmosphere. Although diabetes does not affect intelligence or learning capabilities, sometimes young people with the disorder find that they must work a bit harder than their healthy peers to reach their academic potential. This is true for a number of reasons, one of them being the absences from school caused by illness or doctor's appointments—especially soon after the diagnosis when the person's treatment plans often need frequent adjustments.

TEACHERS—AND ALL ADULTS RESPONSIBLE FOR A YOUNG PERSON'S HEALTH AND WELL-BEING—SHOULD BE INFORMED WHEN A STUDENT HAS DIABETES. THEY SHOULD ALSO KNOW THE SYMPTOMS OF INSULIN REACTIONS OR HIGH BLOOD-SUGAR CRISES, AND SHOULD LEARN WHAT TO DO IN AN EMERGENCY.

Symptoms and side effects also may make learning more difficult. It's almost impossible to concentrate on lessons when insulin reactions occur—even mild ones. In most cases, students with diabetes will need some special consideration from their teachers, school administrators, and fellow students in order to succeed. During one period when Abigail's illness was especially difficult to control, she was forced to stay home more often than was usual. Her teacher gave her extra-credit assignments and take-home quizzes to make up for lost class time.

"A lot of teachers have been great about my diabetes," says Robert, "especially when I was going through some hard times managing and had to take some time out. I even had one teacher who called me on the afternoons I was home to make sure I was up-to-date on the assignments."

Unfortunately, sometimes special attention can be seen as more negative than positive—at least to the student with diabetes. Bonnie's teachers asked her to explain in front of all her classes what diabetes was and what it felt like. Bonnie felt as if "that's all I was—diabetes." With the best of intentions, thirteen-year-old Susan's science teacher announced the fact that Susan had diabetes to the whole class "because he thought we could all learn something about the disease" from her experience. "I guess if I hadn't been going through a down time," Susan remarks, "I might have been flattered that he wanted me to talk about what was going on. Instead, it made me feel weird." Sometimes talking about diabetes is helpful to the person with the illness; sometimes it is not.

There are, apparently, some advantages to having a chronic illness like diabetes. Many children and young adults attain a sense of maturity and sensitivity far beyond their years as a result of coping with their disease. The fact that they are forced to handle both the normal challenges of growing up as well as the challenge of their physical care gives them extra doses of self-discipline.

LEARNING INDEPENDENCE AND SELF-CARE

A person trying to stay in control of diabetes has a lot to think about every day. Whether at school or away from home at a friend's house or at camp, there are some special considerations that a person with diabetes needs to keep in mind in order to stay safe and healthy.

By the time that Bonnie first started sleeping over at friends' houses, she knew how to give herself shots and was comfortable with it. "I made sure that my friends' parents knew everything that was going on, too, so they wouldn't be surprised when I took out my needles. And so they'd know what to do if something went wrong." Eleven-year-old Rachel remarks: "My friends know I have diabetes, and I feel comfortable about that. When I'm at their homes for sleepovers, I give myself my own shot. My mom doesn't have to come over and do it anymore."

There are a few general guidelines for a young person with diabetes to keep in mind when spending time away from home:

• The adults who are supervising should be aware that you have diabetes.

When away from home, a young person with diabetes should wear a Medic Alert bracelet or necklace that has an emergency medical number clearly marked on it.

- You should always wear a bracelet or necklace that indicates that you have diabetes. It should also have an emergency phone number imprinted on it.

- You should feel comfortable about taking care of yourself before you stay away from home for any period. Girls aged nine and boys aged eleven are generally old enough to go on sleepovers or to overnight camp.

Taking on more and more responsibility for self-care is a natural part of growing up. So is thinking about the future. Young people with diabetes may see the future a bit differently than their peers do: Some feel that because of the potential for complications—no matter how well they take care of themselves—there is no point in really working to maintain their health. Even if doctors prove to them that good control minimizes complications later on, they may still decide that taking care of themselves is just too much trouble. Probably all people with diabetes feel this way at one time or another. But these young adults are dealing with feelings of anger, guilt, resentment, sadness, or other strong and often conflicting emotions—emotions they need to take responsibility for and work out in order to have a healthy, happy life.

Chapter Six

HOPE FOR THE FUTURE

Young people with diabetes can learn to help themselves cope with their illness. Friends and family can help, too, and so can the many scientists and researchers who are constantly investigating ways to improve diabetes care as well as searching for a cure in laboratories across the United States and around the world.

Scientists and physicians have made great progress in the area of diabetes care since the discovery of insulin more than seventy years ago. Since then, diabetes specialists have developed a number of innovative products and techniques that directly aid people in the daily management of their disease. In addition to improving day-to-day care, several organizations and groups aggressively campaign for funds for research. Research is conducted in two main areas: how to prevent the disease and how to cure it.

There are also a number of organizations that provide emotional, physical, and social support to young adults with diabetes and to their families. The future of diabetes management looks brighter every day.

PREVENTING DIABETES

In the past, doctors thought that diabetes developed rapidly once symptoms first appeared. Further research, however, showed that diabetes actually develops slowly and over a long period of time. As discussed in Chapter 1, some scientists believe that Type I diabetes results from an autoimmune disorder in which the body's immune-system cells destroy certain cells in the pancreas. This process can take several years without producing any outward symptoms of the disease. By the time symptoms appear, most of the damage has been done. With this knowledge, scientists are looking for ways to stop the disease in its earliest stages, before permanent damage to the pancreas and metabolism can occur.

Several strategies for early detection are being considered:

- *Screening tests:* Scientists are developing screening tests—special laboratory tests that examine blood components—that would identify those young people who are at highest risk for developing Type I diabetes. Although many young people are the first in their families to develop the disease, a young person with a family history of the disorder is more liable to develop the disease than someone without such a history. These tests are extremely expensive and time-consuming, and thus appropriate only for those young people who have a long and extensive history of diabetes in their family. Nevertheless, medical professionals remain hopeful that in the future a diabetes screening test will be administered at birth as part of the regular blood testing.

- *Insulin treatments:* Once a doctor determines that a young person is at risk for developing diabetes, the doctor has the option of prescribing doses of insulin to try to stop the progression of the disease. In one study, a medical team offered preventive insulin to a group of twelve "prediabetic" relatives of patients with diabetes. Seven declined the treatment, and five decided to try it. At the end of three years, all seven of those who decided not to take the insulin had developed Type I diabetes, while only two in the other group became ill.

• *Vaccines:* The success that scientists have had with preventive insulin has led to a search for another type of prevention strategy. One popular theory as to why insulin treatments work is that injected insulin immunizes the body against an attack on its own beta cells. If this theory is true, researchers believe they can develop a standard vaccination that would prevent the destructive process from ever beginning.

• *Anti-rejection medications:* A drug called cyclosporine is also being investigated. Cyclosporine appears to restore beta-cell function to some degree. This medication may also delay the onset of diabetes, postponing the disease for several years for those young people destined to develop it. Unfortunately, drugs like cyclosporine also have unpleasant side effects, including the destruction of healthy cells and damage to body tissues and organs. Thus the search for an effective prevention strategy is not yet over.

PREVENTING COMPLICATIONS, IMPROVING CARE

Scientists, doctors, and researchers aren't certain that they will one day be able to prevent diabetes. In the meantime, however, they have developed several ways to make daily management of the disease easier and to decrease the likelihood of future complications. In fact, the most effective way for those with diabetes to reduce the risk of developing complications in the future is to take care of themselves—and the easier it is to take care of themselves, the more likely it is that young people will be able to effectively manage their own health.

Doctors perform one of three types of screening tests on individuals they consider to be at high risk for developing type I diabetes.

• The patient does not eat for several hours. Then the doctor gives the patient something to eat and measures the patient's blood sugar for several hours after digestion begins.

• The doctor gives the patient a very sweet drink, then checks the patient's blood-sugar levels every hour for several hours.

• The doctor takes blood tests every month for several months to measure blood-sugar levels, then averages the results of the tests.

Here are several of the new daily-care methods that scientists have developed to make life easier for people with diabetes today and in the future:

• *Drugs to treat complications:* Ideally, good diabetes control and care during childhood and adolescence reduce the likelihood that complications will develop later in life. Researchers are studying various medications, such as Capoten, that will help slow the progression of complications, particularly kidney disease.

• *Laser surgery:* Laser surgery has revolutionized a number of medical procedures, making everything from knee surgery to gallbladder operations easier and safer to perform. Sophisticated laser surgery now significantly reduces the chances of blindness caused by retina damage in people with diabetes.

- *Blood-glucose machines:* Blood-glucose machines quickly measure the amount of glucose in the blood. With these devices, people can find out their exact blood-sugar level at any moment, which allows them greater freedom in planning their meals and physical activities.

- *Insulin pumps:* An insulin pump automatically releases insulin into the blood at regular intervals. This may seem like a good alternative to injections, but some people report that the device (which is worn by the user) feels bulky, and that its cord, which carries insulin into the body, occasionally gets jammed, twisted, and stuck. The pump is still convenient for people who have busy schedules and need a great deal of flexibility and freedom in their treatment program.

- *Artificial or transplanted pancreas:* Researchers are developing an artificial pancreas that, when placed into the body, would automatically release the correct amount of insulin. Scientists have also explored the possibility of transplanting healthy pancreatic cells from one person into a person with diabetes. Unfortunately, there are potential problems with this form of treatment because one person's body often rejects tissue from another's.

- *Implants:* Scientists are testing a special kind of implant that would be placed under a person's skin, measure blood-sugar levels, then draw the needed amount of insulin from a pump that has also been placed under the skin. The pump would eliminate the need for glucose testing and insulin injections, while maintaining even, healthy levels of insulin and glucose circulating in the blood. So far, however, this method of treatment remains highly experimental and is not yet available.

HOPE FOR A CURE

When will there be a cure for diabetes? No doctor or scientist can yet provide an answer to this question, and most believe it is more important for people with diabetes to take good care of themselves everyday than to focus their hopes on an elusive cure. Experts agree that diabetes is a very complicated disease, one that will be difficult to cure. Researchers continue to work, however, on more effective types of insulin, noninvasive monitors, and even computers that determine insulin doses. They continue to work to make care easier while still searching for a cure.

For many people with diabetes, the hope for a cure gives them encouragement that one day they may no longer have to give themselves injections, monitor their blood, or worry about complications. Eleven-year-old Rachel says: "When I take part in a walk-a-thon to raise money for a cure, I feel like I'm doing something to help not only myself, but everyone with diabetes." By actively working for a cure, whether in a walk-a-thon or as a participant in a scientific study, young people often feel that they are helping to make a difference in their own futures.

NO ONE HAS TO BE ALONE

All the different treatment techniques, prevention options, and drug therapies available to people with diabetes can be very confusing. Most people with diabetes have felt alone and isolated at some point while coping with their illness. Finding support is vital to leading a happy and fulfilling life.

Diabetes camps provide a supportive environment in which young people with diabetes can make new friends and have fun.

Fortunately, there are a number of people, groups, and organizations that help young adults and their families learn more about the disease, meet other children and families with diabetes, and sponsor exciting activities and events.

Doctors, nurses, and social workers are some of the most effective and accessible sources of information and support for children and adolescents with diabetes.

Many young people with diabetes enjoy a few weeks away from their families each summer at camps designed specifically to meet their needs. There are two diabetes camps in the United States: the Clara Barton camp for girls in Oxford, Massachusetts, and the Joslin Camp for boys in Charlton, Massachusetts. Patients are admitted upon recommendation by their doctors.

At a diabetes camp, young people are surrounded by others who have the same concerns they do. They can learn from each other and share in a supportive, open, and fun environment. Susan says of her few weeks at camp: "I loved it. The whole schedule was geared around our needs as people with diabetes. . . everyone there had to inject themselves, monitor their blood-sugar levels, and watch what they ate." Rachel, who went to camp for the first time a couple of years ago, comments: "I had a wonderful time because I found out that I wasn't the only one, that there are millions of kids like me and we can do what all other kids do at camp, like ride horses and swim."

CAMPS FOR PEOPLE WITH DIABETES OFFER THE SAME ACTIVITIES AS REGULAR CAMPS, BUT ARE STAFFED AND ATTENDED BY PEOPLE WITH DIABETES. IN THESE CAMPS, YOUNG ADULTS HAVE AN OPPORTUNITY TO MEET HUNDREDS OF OTHER KIDS WHO ARE FACING THE SAME CHALLENGES.

When young people feel alone or lost, they may turn to a friend for advice and comfort. Often those with diabetes feel that because their friends don't have the disease, they cannot understand their situation and so decide not to burden them with their problems. Buddy programs, many of which are sponsored by hospitals, medical schools, and private organizations, pair up young adults with diabetes or chronic illnesses so that they each have someone to confide in, someone who truly understands the challenges they face. Buddies are usually similar in age, so they share similar perspectives on family, school, and friends. Sometimes, a person with diabetes is paired with someone with a different chronic illness. This way, each can each learn that he or she is not alone and that millions of children have lifelong conditions and face similar challenges. The two buddies are also able to compare and contrast their different conditions and their coping strategies.

There are as many ways of coping with chronic illnesses as there are young people who suffer from them. One group of kids with diabetes made an educational video to explain who they were and how the illness affected their lives. Twelve-year-old Mark, a participant in the production, says: "I made the video with other kids. We talk about how we live with diabetes, how we participate in physical activities, what our diets are like. We even interviewed a bunch of people to see what they knew about diabetes."

Bonnie, one of Mark's video partners, says: "The best thing about diabetes is that, even though you have a disease, you get to enjoy a lot of stuff other kids don't. The video we made gets shown across the country and was a lot of fun to make." Making the video gave Mark, Bonnie, and their co-stars an opportunity to convey information about themselves, while inspiring others to become involved with diabetes in new and creative ways.

Casey Johnson and her parents had another idea: to write a book about their experiences. *Managing Your Child's Diabetes* tells the story of both Casey's experiences with the illness and those of her parents. By writing down their thoughts, fears, and concerns, they all found it easier to cope with their day-to-day challenges. Casey says:

We wrote the book in 1992, and it was a public-service idea. I was in the hospital when I was eight, and there were no good books that I could read or

that my mother could read that explained every-
thing. What was available were medical textbooks
that were like five thousand pages long and had
words you couldn't understand unless you were a
doctor. We thought, "Wouldn't it be great to have
a book that you could understand when you were
in the first stages of the disease?" There was noth-
ing like that at the time I was diagnosed.

Casey also says that one of the things that made her feel better about having diabetes, and more hopeful about the future, was knowing that actors like Mary Tyler Moore and James Cagney, and sports figures like hockey star Bobby Clarke and football player Jonathan Hayes all have diabetes. Historical figures, such as Thomas Edison, Paul Cézanne, and Fiorello LaGuardia, rose to great heights of accomplishment while coping with diabetes.

Needless to say, not everyone has the time, resources, or desire to make videos or write books, but there are many other ways that young people who wish to can learn more and teach others about the disease.

Some young adults and their families decide not to surround themselves with other people with diabetes, but instead feel more comfortable coping with the illness alone. But most people do seek some form of support and guidance, especially when diabetes first becomes part of their lives. Luckily, there are not only in-hospital support services to help families adjust, but there are also national and international organizations that provide a network of services and events that connect young people and their families with others having similar concerns.

There are four major organizations that provide information and resources to people with diabetes. Some of these organizations bring children, young adults, and their families together by offering a variety of activities, including walk-a-thons, carnivals, and educational programs.

American Diabetes Association
P.O. Box 25757
1660 Duke Street
Alexandria, VA 22314

International Diabetic Athletes Association (IDAA)
1931 East Rovey Avenue
Phoenix, AZ 85016

Joslin Diabetes Center
1 Joslin Place
Boston, MA 02215

Juvenile Diabetes Foundation International
432 Park Avenue South
New York, NY 10016-8013

While performing all of the tasks of caring for themselves physically, people with diabetes must also deal with the frustrations and difficulties of staying in control when it sometimes seems impossible. The many support systems that exist, whether provided by a medical professional or a large organization, offer the advice, knowledge, and comfort necessary for a person to manage a chronic illness like diabetes.

The many voices that tell the stories in this book teach us an important lesson: Whether or not scientists find a cure in the near future, people who learn to cope with the changes and challenges that diabetes presents—by caring for themselves and by reaching out to others—can lead healthy, joyful, and fulfilling lives.

GLOSSARY

Adult-onset diabetes: Type II or non-insulin-dependent diabetes.

Autoimmune disorder: A disease or disorder in which a person's immune system attacks healthy as well as unhealthy parts of the body.

Beta cells: The cells in the pancreas responsible for producing insulin. In a person with Type I diabetes, most beta cells have been destroyed.

Blood-glucose monitoring: The measuring of blood-sugar levels, using one of several methods and devices, including home-testing kits.

Carbohydrates: Common name for starches and sugars that the body converts to glucose for energy.

Chronic illness: A disease that lasts for many years, perhaps a lifetime.

Circulatory system: The system, including veins and arteries, by which blood circulates through the body.

Coma: The state of being unconscious. Diabetic comas can be due to a high or low blood-glucose level.

Diabetes mellitus: A disease caused by the body's inability to convert carbohydrates to glucose due to a lack of insulin.

Diabetic coma: See *Ketoacidosis*.

Endocrine system: A network of glands that secrete hormones into the bloodstream, which controls various body processes.

Endocrinologist: A doctor who specializes in the treatment of disorders related to hormones, including diabetes.

Fat: An organic substance found in such foods as oils, dairy products, meats, seeds, and nuts.

Fatty acid: A basic unit of fat, such as butyric acid, which is found in butter. When the body lacks glucose, the body burns fatty acids for energy.

Glucose: The simple blood sugar that the body converts into energy.

Glycogen: A complex carbohydrate stored in the liver and muscles and released when glucose is needed by cells for energy.

Heredity: The passing of a trait genetically from parent to child.

Hyperglycemia: A condition in which there is too much sugar in the bloodstream and blood-glucose levels are higher than normal. A person without diabetes has a normal blood-glucose level that ranges from 70 to 130 milligrams of sugar per milliliter of blood. A person with diabetes may have 300 or more milligrams of sugar per milliliter of blood.

Hypoglycemia: A condition in which the blood-glucose level is lower than normal. See also *Hyperglycemia.*

Insulin: A hormone, secreted by the beta cells of the pancreas, which regulates the movement of glucose from the blood to the body cells.

Insulin-dependent diabetes: A chronic condition in which the pancreas makes little or no insulin. This type of diabetes requires manufactured insulin as treatment. Also known as Type I or juvenile-onset diabetes.

Insulin reaction: A reaction that occurs when there is too low a level of glucose in the blood (hypoglycemia) and can be caused when a person with diabetes either injects too much insulin, eats too little food, or exercises without having eaten enough food. Symptoms include hunger, nausea, weakness, and confusion.

Juvenile-onset diabetes: Type I or insulin-dependent diabetes.

Ketoacidosis: A condition that occurs when blood-glucose levels become dangerously high. Also known as diabetic coma.

Ketones: Substances formed when body cells use fatty acids for energy because there is an insufficient amount of glucose.

Neuropathy: A condition that occurs when nerves in the

body are damaged by high blood pressure. Symptoms may include loss of sensation, tingling, and/or pain.

Non-insulin-dependent diabetes: A condition that usually develops in people after age forty. This type of diabetes is managed with proper diet and exercise. Also known as Type II or adult-onset diabetes.

Nutritionist: A person trained to plan healthy and beneficial diets and eating programs.

Pancreas: The gland behind the stomach that produces the hormone insulin as well as secretes a digestive fluid called pancreatic juice.

Pancreatic transplant: An experimental surgical procedure that involves replacing the pancreas of a person with diabetes with a healthy pancreas that can make insulin.

Protein: A nitrogen-containing food that is essential to the repair and growth of body tissue. After water, it is the second most plentiful substance in the body.

Retina: The light-sensitive area at the back of the eye that contains many small blood vessels.

Retinopathy: An eye disease caused, in part, by lack of oxygen in the eye. Damage to the retina occurs when the small blood vessels enlarge and leak fluid into the center of the retina; a common complication of diabetes.

Type I diabetes: See *Insulin-dependent diabetes.*

Type II diabetes: See *Non-insulin-dependent diabetes.*

FURTHER READING

Beaser, M.S., and the staff at the Joslin Diabetes Center. *Outsmarting Diabetes*. Boston: Joslin Diabetes Center, 1994.

Dolger, Henry, M.D., and Bernard Seeman. *How to Live with Diabetes*. New York: Pyramid Books, 1975.

Edelwich, Jerry, and Archie Brodsky. *Diabetes: Caring for Your Emotions as Well as Your Health*. Reading, MA: Addison-Wesley, 1986.

Johnson, Robert Wood, IV, Casey Johnson, Sale Johnson, and Susan Kleinman. *Managing Your Child's Diabetes*. New York: MasterMedia Limited, 1994.

Juliano, Joseph, M.D. *When Diabetes Complicates Your Life*. Minneapolis: CHRONIMED Publishing, 1993.

Kipnis, Lynne, and Susan Adler. *You Can't Catch Diabetes from a Friend*. Gainesville, FL: Triad Scientific Publishers, 1979.

Little, Marjorie. *The Encyclopedia of Health: Diabetes*. New York: Chelsea House Publishers, 1991.

Riedman, Sarah R. *Diabetes*. New York: Franklin Watts, 1980.

Silverstein, Alvin and Virginia B. *The Sugar Disease: Diabetes*. New York: J. B. Lippincott, 1980.

INDEX